CW01496307

The Honest Handbooks

The Simple Rules of Getting A Lot Done

Proven and actionable rules to boost your productivity and achieve more everyday

Victor SIXTIN

Copyright

The Simple Rules of Getting A Lot Done

Also in *The Honest Handbooks* series

The Simple Rules of Project Management,
Victor Sixtin

About *The Honest Handbooks*

The Honest Handbooks are a series of useful books for professionals. They are books that get straight to the point, with clear, actionable recommendations based on years of experience in trenches.

In a nutshell: what you should know when taking on a new job.

There are thousands of clever management/business/leadership/self-development books written by smart people. They develop and present around three to six main ideas and spread them out over hundreds of pages.

After hours of reading, you hopefully get the big picture, but you have no clue where to start if you want to implement part or all of it.

The *Honest Handbooks* are the exact opposite: short, easy-to-read books with clear step-by-step actions to take right away. Every book can be read in two hours or less. They are based on practical rules with short, detailed instructions for implementation.

Once you've read each rule's section, take a moment to reflect and imagine how you could put it into practice. The information is accessible and designed to encourage the reader to refer back to it often and read it over and over again.

The *Honest Handbooks* are not written by journalists or scholars (bless their hearts).

Preface to The Simple Rules of Getting A Lot Done

I'm not a start-up guru nor a TED Talk speaker. I don't wake up at 5 a.m. to run 10k on the beach before meditating. I'm a regular corporate guy, not here to change your life with revolutionary concepts, but simply to try to help with good advice that comes from practical experience.

You won't find me on linked-in. I maintain anonymity as I am still actively employed in the field. I want to protect my position at my current employer, along with my freedom to be able to write what I want.

Here's my background.

Trained in engineering, I started as a consultant in business strategy and transformation, supporting various companies on digital, client, and distribution matters. This experience sharpened my ability to deliver exceptional work, take charge of expansive projects, and lead sizable teams effectively.

A big international retailer asked me then to help plan its digital transformation and helm a series of major innovation projects. Working with this $100 billion company, I developed a nuanced understanding of corporate dynamics and the art of steering through the complex governance of large organizations.

Most recently, I've served as the head of digital and innovation at a worldwide product company. Our work in designing, building, and selling products has been met with tremendous success, generating tens of billions in revenue and sustaining a healthy profit margin. In this conservative, because very successful, company, I've mastered the nuances of being a persuasive change agent, driving innovation and progress.

In my personal life, I'm a happy husband and father of two daughters. I love to have a great work-life balance to have time for my friends and family and sports.

This book is a distillation of my experiences, a testament to the power of *Project Management* and how it changes the world.

The simple rules of Getting A Lot Done

The Honest Handbooks

Introduction

You see, in this world, there is two kinds of people, my friend: those who deliver and those who don't.

But be careful, being productive is not necessarily a blessing.

First, being delivery oriented can drive you nuts when you're trapped in the middle of slow people. You'll spend hours and hours in meeting trying to catalyze everyone towards action. The worst scenario is being managed by someone slow.

Second, getting things done or not does not define your level of success. Lots of people who don't deliver get promoted. They may be good at communication and at navigating company politics. In a company, there's no point in delivering things no one is aware of. You will quickly notice, or maybe you already have, that some people deliver very little, but they manage to make it look big.

But even if it does not predict your level of happiness, being able to get a lot done will give you the opportunity to hold the reins of your life.

Gentle warning: if you don't change how you live or work, you'll end up with the same results.

This book has been written for those who want to improve their lives.

If you're happy with what you have, don't bother reading this book. Just enjoy life. Don't try to fix what's not broken. Be yourself, the way you are today and be happy for the rest of your life.

If you feel like you might need to change

something, this book is for you. Lots of people struggle with productivity. We procrastinate. In our professional life but also in our personal life. We watch a quick video on YouTube. We cannot help ourselves from clicking on the next episode button. We look at our phones every minute to see if we have a new message or a new notification. We're falling for immediate pleasures, that in the end slow down our progress in life.

The irony is that being more productive would help us deliver more so we could have more free time and more fun.

Reading this book is a good start if you want to do more and waste less time. We have a limited number of hours to live, let's not waste them.

But just reading this book won't help you. But putting it into action and living according to the rules I recommend certainly will.

It's very simple, no excuses.

In this 2023 edition, I've added 4 rules to the original ones. There are 38 rules. Each one is self-speaking and there's less than a page in development.

Most of the rules may seem obvious, and you will think, "Thank you mister obvious". But every time you think that, take a moment to reflect and see if you're really doing it. For example, when I advise you to take minutes for every meeting, reflect on the percentage of the meetings you attend where someone is assigned the task of taking minutes and distributing them to the attendees. Whatever the answer, your next action will be to improve that percentage.

I recommend reading this book either at the very beginning or the very end of the day. Read two to four rules at a time and then take a minute to imagine what it would look and feel like if you applied them perfectly as directed. Now take the recommended steps to implement each rule in your professional and personal life.

When you have read all the rules, start again from the beginning. Iterate this process until you're comfortable with your degree of implementation of every rule.
Come back to it once a year.

The rules may be simple and straightforward. But if you were already doing them all, you wouldn't be reading this book. Your job is to take action, implement them all and apply them every day.

If you have no intention to implement the rules, you're better off stopping right here. Don't waste your time reading these rules.

Only by changing the way you act, will you have different results.

The Simple Rules of Getting A Lot Done

1

Quit Social Media

All types of social media are black holes that suck your time and motivation.

They are truly design marvels.

They are engineered to keep you glued to your phone as long as possible. Their business model is ads, so basically their only goal is to keep you distracted, to keep you scrolling endlessly like a zombie. They invented clever vanity metrics like likes or followers to gamify the experience to keep you coming back often to check how you're doing.

You can't blame them, like you can't blame fries for being tasty. If you start a diet, you know you must quit eating fries. If you want to take control of your time, the first thing to do is quit all social media.

Even if you are a content creator. Create off social media. Just connect to drop your nugget on your favorite platform and leave.

Anyone who uninstalls all the social media apps from their smartphone will instantly improve their productivity by at least 20%.

2

Have Clear Priorities

At this very moment, do you know the three most important things for you?

Not everything we do is important. Be clear-minded about what is important for you in both your professional and personal life. On a short term and on a long term.

On a long term, what do you want to be remembered for? Do you want to be a visionary entrepreneur? Or a loving wife/husband, mother/father or friend? There is no good or bad answer but not having an aswer is not good.

On the short term, what must you deliver in the three next months? Close a deal? Recruit a new employee? Plan a seminar? Organize a birthday party? Book a vacation?

At the beginning of every month, write down your projects, your wills and your desires, everything you have on your mind.

Think wide: job, family, friends, hobbies, charities, etc. Rank the list from the most important to the least important. And then stick to it.

If your month's top priority is your wife's birthday party, start every day by checking off the next action steps for it to be a success. Choosing it as your top priority means that if your boss calls you for an extra that will keep you busy so you can't stay on top of the party planning details, you will turn him down. That's what sticking to your priorities means.

Write your top five priorities for the month

on a post it and stick-it somewhere where you'll see it every day.

3

Break Down Things into Actionable Steps

(The 15 Minute Rule)

We often procrastinate because our goals and tasks to do are too general.

Success is ensured when we have specific, actionable goals we can break down into small, easy to accomplish steps.

Let's say that one of your goals is, "I'd like to learn to play the guitar".

Sounds good, but if you have this on your to do list, you're most likely going to end up procrastinating by watching a video of Prince on YouTube.

But once you put something specific on your to-do list like, "Sign up for a beginner's guitar lesson at the music shop a few blocks from your office", you're more likely to do it.

For everything you want to achieve, you must identify the first small actionable steps. What is the succession of small actions that will slowly bring you closer to your goal?
A simple rule of thumb is "the 15 minutes rule": if a task will take more than 15 minutes, break it down into smaller chunks before adding them to your to-do list.

Amazing things begin by completing one small step.

4

If It's Quick, Do It Now

(The 2 Minutes Rule)

Examine your To-Do List made up of actionable steps (see rule #1).
Look for tasks that take less than two minutes to do, do the first one now.

In fact, you shouldn't even put these quick tasks on your to-do list you should just do them immediately.
There could be some exceptions to this rule, like if you have to call someone and the person in on vacation, but these instances are rare.

Full disclosure, this rule and the previous one are greatly inspired by the jewel from Tony Allen: *Getting Things Done*. It's a must read for managing your to-do list.

5

Procrastinate

You're probably surprised I'm telling you to procrastinate. Since my advice goes against everything you've heard, right?

The rule should be "procrastinate on taking actions that aren't important" but it's less catchy.
Yes, procrastination is actually a good thing when it frees up time for your priorities.

Procrastinate means postponing it until later. The "until later" is important. Procrastinating is not cancelling.
Is there a YouTube video you want to watch but now is not a good time? Add it to your

to-do list with a lower priority. It's okay to have fun, you'll watch it during a low intensity moment of your day or week. Don't cancel fun, less important things or you'll just set yourself up for feeling resentful of your priorities or like you're missing out.

Master your time, prioritize doing the most important things during your high productivity times, make time for fun later.

There's another case where procrastinating can be beneficial: when you're not ready to move forward on a project or task because it requires further thought or development. Sometimes you must spend more time thinking about an idea before being able to carry out the tasks to achieve it in an efficient way. You don't know exactly what you want to do and that's okay for now. You'll think about it while you're running, cooking or taking a shower and quickly you'll have a better idea of what you want to achieve. At that point, you'll be able to identify the very best next steps to deliver it.

6

Let's Pomodoro

(Focus for Short Periods of Time)

Today, our over stimulated brains can only focus for 15 minutes maximum. After that, your capacity to stay focused and resist notifications from your devices or input from your environment is close to zero.

So the best way to be productive is to embrace that fact and to find a good balance between focused action and relaxation. Work for 15 minutes, relax for 5 minutes.

Start a timer for 15 minutes and block out everything else. Don't read any notifications, don't answer your phone, don't switch your browser tabs, don't change the music you're listening to or better don't listen to any music. Just focus.

When the timer rings, finish up what you were doing. Then start a timer for five minutes and do what you want: catch-up on your notifications, watch YouTube, pee, grab a coffee, walk around the office…

When the timer rings, start another timer for 15 minutes and focus.

Every six cycles (around 1 hour and a half), take a break for 15 to 30 minutes. There's only one non-negotiable rule here: get-up and walk, preferably outside to give yourself some time away from your office.

7

Every Action Must Have a Deliverable

Whatever you do, something must come out of it: a note, a phone call, an email, a Power-Point, some code, etc.

If you're just brainstorming, scribble something down on a post-it. If you're searching for gift ideas, make a list of options. If you're reflecting on how you could structure a speech, draft a PowerPoint.

Why is this essential?

First, when you come back to it later, you'll be happy you've already gotten started and can build on it. As a result you'll have good results faster.

Second, writing or sketching something will force you to synthesize and to articulate what you're working on.

Otherwise, after putting in an hour of work, if you haven't created anything, it's like you didn't do anything. And that's not true. So make sure you give yourself credit for everything you do by creating something tangible.

8

Create Long Work Blocks in Your Schedule

Even if every task on your to-do list only takes 15 minutes to complete, it's often better to be able to complete similar tasks one right after another.

If you want to be able to dedicate one or two hours to a single project, the only way for most of us to accomplish it is to book a slot on the calendar. If you don't block off dedicated time to devote to the single task, you'll end up spending the same amount of time on checking your emails and completing one or two small tasks related to different topics.

Have you heard the big rocks small rocks metaphor?

"A teacher asks one of his students to fill a jar with rocks of different sizes and sand. The student starts by pouring the sand in the jar. Then the small rocks. When he tries to add the big rocks, the jar is already full. So the teacher empties the jar. Then he put the big rocks in first. Next he adds the small rocks that fill in between the big ones. Last, he adds the sand that fills the last empty spaces between the small rocks."

The lesson here is you must start with important tasks, you must put them on your schedule first. Then you can add the secondary projects. And you will always find time for the small stuff.

9

Don't Hesitate to Refuse a Meeting Request

Whatever your title or your experience, your presence is not essential in every meeting.

Before accepting any meeting request, ask what's on the agenda. If you can delegate the meeting to someone more involved in the projects being discussed, do it! Turn it down. You can always still read the minutes.

And don't make this classic mistake: "If I'm not relevant, I'll work on something else": you won't be as productive as being at your desk and you won't make a good impression at the meeting if you are not participating and focused. If you attend, you have to be 100% focused. Attend or don't attend, there is no "in between".

There are red flags to help you decide which meetings to decline:
Decline any meeting without an agenda.
Decline any meeting without preread.
Decline any follow-up meeting if there are no minutes of the previous one.

Life's too short to waste it in lousy meetings.

10

Start Every Meeting with the agenda or the Minutes of the Last One

At this point, if you're in a meeting it's because the agenda is clear and you have some value to add.

Enjoy the small talk at the beginning. It's important to genuinely connect with your peers. Try to catch-up with everyone. It will also give you hints about the mood of the meeting.

After a couple of minutes, start the meeting and try to get straight to the point. If you're not leading the meeting, wait for the organizer to introduce the meeting and present the agenda.

Do not waste too much time reframing a context everyone should be aware of. Dedicate your time to tackling the current challenges being faced.

Of course, if it's a follow-up, you must start with the minutes of the previous meeting and the actions that were listed.

Don't be shy to show that you're action oriented and that you'd like to keep it as short as possible.

11

Write Minutes for Every Meeting

No exceptions.

Having a work meeting without assigning someone to take minutes relies on the hope that everybody is diligent. Be ready to be disappointed. Not everyone has a good memory, not everyone is well organized. Hope is not a good strategy.

It's also important to remember what has been said and decided in order not to waste time by having the same discussion again later.

Even if you're not the organizer of the meeting, write dows your own minutes. You can choose whether to share them or not but be sure to take notes for yourself.

Note the main issues, the different scenarios discussed, the decisions made and the next actions.

12

Say No

It's hard to say no.

Everybody wants to please their manager, their friend and their peers. But you end up with too much on your plate, unable to deliver everything and disappointing people.

Imagine you've invited someone for a drink. He or she says yes. You've been waiting for them at the bar for two hours and they never show up. Then you receive a text: "Sorry, too many things to do, unable to make it". How do you feel? Wouldn't you have preferred a straight "No sorry, too busy at the moment"? You would have had a better evening and wouldn't feel like you wasted your time.

When someone asks you to do something, the first question to ask yourself is: Do I have the capacity (time, resources, expertise) to do it?

If you don't, you have to assess this request regarding your current priorities: is this more important?

(Hint : sometimes it's your boss who will say it's more important than what you consider your top priority)

There are two possibilities.

Either it's important, and you can add it to your to-do list and remove something else.

Or it's not important, and you can just say NO.

You have to stay focused on your priorities and protect yourself from any distractions.

It can be a gentle, clean "no".

Or it can be a subtle more ambiguous "I'll think about it".

13

Don't Think, Do

Just do it.
Sounds familiar?

Many people think. They can think for a long time. Imagining different ways to do it. Weighing the pros and the cons. Questioning. Overthinking. In the end, nothing happens and there are no results.

Don't think, do.
Don't wait to do it until it's perfect in your head, because it will never be, you will never know the results if you do nothing.
Do it once. If it's not good, do it again. Each time you iterate you will learn. What works,

what doesn't. What can be done, what can't.
What's cheap, what's expensive.

Iterate until you're satisfied.
Often, things are better done than perfect.

14

Ignorance or Inexperience Are Not Valid Excuses

Not doing anything or procrastinating because you don't know how to do it is inexcusable.

This is the age of information.
Don't know how to do something? Google it! I have never thought of a question someone else hadn't already asked before on the internet. It's even scary.
You will find tutorials, forums and videos that will explain how to do anything you want to learn.

The Simple Rules of Getting A Lot Done

It has never been this easy to learn or to find someone to help you.

Try and you will learn.

15

Share Your Ideas, Ask for Advice

Some people are afraid to be vulnerable. They don't share their feelings and their ideas. They are afraid to be challenged.
They prefer to work on their ideas on their own. However, when they unveil it, they discover that their work does not fully meet the requirements or that they could have done it in a different, better way.

The most impressive people I meet do not hesitate to be open and to share what they have in mind. No matter your paygrade.
When they have something in mind, they

want to refine it, to expose it to different points of view so that they can improve it.

Nobody will steal your idea.

16

Don't Listen to Others Too Much

There's a time for discussion. And there's a time for action.

Share, open-up to others, ask for advice and what traps to avoid. Listen to what people might say. Then you can choose to follow their advice or do it your own way. Do not make the same mistake others did before, but you're also not obliged to do exactly what they did even if they succeeded.

Once you have gotten some feedback and some advice, start. Draft or prototype something. In this way, should you need additional inputs, you'll have something to show to others. It will be easier to correct and to iterate.

17

Set Deadlines

Deadlines are underrated.

They are only seen as constraints, as additional pressure.

By design, you can't be late if there's no deadline.
However, they are an interesting tool to add some gentle pressure on you in order to help you become a little more focused and productive.

But deadlines are also a great tool to help you organize your work and your priorities. Setting deadlines for each of your tasks will help you identify congestion zones. It's not possible to deliver everything at the same time.

Take some time to identify what could be a good delivery date for each of your tasks. Then break down the work into smaller chunks in order to limit stress areas and to limit late delivery.

18

Commit with
Other People

Have you ever launched into a crazy challenge? Like doing a marathon?
Or way more common, have you ever tried to go on a diet or to start going to the gym? Have you noticed that your level of commitment is directly related to the number of people you told about your goal?

Social pressure is powerful.

Tell everyone that you're going to do something, and you can be sure that you'll have regular requests for updates. You don't want to disappoint the people around you so that social pressure will give you a gentle pressure to deliver.

Share what you're up to with your social circle, from small to crazy things, and you'll immediately increase your chances of success.

19

Surround Yourself
with the Best

Many people are afraid of being outper-
formed by others. It obviously stems from a
lack of confidence. It also reflects a lack of
wisdom.

If you're talented, you know that with access
to other skilled people and resources, you'll
be able to deliver more.

If you're mediocre, you know you'll need to
partner with other more talented people to
do something great.

Smart people know how to stand on the
shoulders of giants.

When you surround yourself with a bunch of crappy people, you will deliver crap.

The best executives of our time have one point in common: they know how to spot and how to poach talented people. They know, the more talents they have, the more they'll deliver and the better they'll deliver.

20

Delegate & Empower

When you have people on your team, it's your job to keep them busy with relevant actions. They've been hired for a reason, and they thrive by delivering. When something lands on your to-do list and it can be handled by someone on your team, delegate.

Delegation is good, empowerment is even better. While delegation means the routing of a simple action, empowerment means trusting someone to tackle an entire project and giving her or him the resources to be successful. By doing so, you will develop your team, they will expand their skills and deliver higher-quality results one after the other.

Finally, if the person on your team that would have been perfect for a job can't do it for any reason, say no or delay. It's your job to protect your team and not overwhelm them.

21

Outsource

Time is money, money is others' time.
When you don't have any time to do something, but you have some money, outsource.

Often people have a limited amount of time
and skills to dedicate to a task. They assume,
they'll do the best they can in the time they
have, and it will be ok.
But if they would have hired someone else
instead; they would have gotten way better results. They would have made a bigger
impact, and the return on investment would
have been incredible. The small amount of
money they invested would have led to big
results.

Don't have the time to prepare slides for your next leadership team presentation? Hire an agency.

Don't have the time to scope this strategic project? Hire a consulting firm.

Don't have the time or the expertise to fix your plumbing? Hire a contractor.

Of course, it takes a little knowledge in what you want to do to be sure you're not over-paying. But once you've seen the impact of something done by a professional, next time you won't hesitate to outsource.

22

Start Small, Every Day

Dreams do not turn into reality overnight.

It often takes a lot of small steps to reach your goals (and the journey is actually more important than the destination but we'll save that for another book).
The hard thing is it's often difficult to see the effects of your actions. Take learning how to play the guitar for example: how many days of practice will it take to feel comfortable with your new skills?

To tackle those big missions and achieve our big dreams, which are often very important and defining for us, the key is consistency:

start small but do something every day that will get you closer to what you truly want.

The path may be long, but the actions are clear and easy. The sooner you begin, the sooner you'll deliver something great.

In the end, it's not that hard to reach your goals. Whatever you've always wanted to do, get started today and work towards it for five minutes. Just five full minutes. And to-morrow work on it again for five minutes. And continue to work on it for five minutes every day for the next month. You can take one day off per week but that's all. You'll be amazed at how much progress you've made toward your goal by the end of the month.

23

Hack Your Routines

Habits are great but they are hard to start and develop. A great way to develop one's ability to master habits is to hack your routines.

Routines are a succession of actions you do every day, at a specific time. For example, every night you go to the toilet then you brush your teeth then you put your pajamas on then you go to bed, and you start to read this book. That's your bedtime routine.

What if you added a small action in between one of those steps? Like write a paragraph of the book you've always wanted to write. Just do it in between the putting on your pajamas step and the getting into bed step. When you finish your workday, put your computer on your bedside table. And when you get into bed, take 15 minutes to write something. In a couple of days, you'll have a few pages. In a month, a chapter. In a year, your book will be finished.

Look through your day and identify all your routines. When you want to start a new habit but can't seem to get motivated to get started, hack one of your routines. In between steps that you're already in the habit of doing every day is where the magic happens.

24

What You Measure Is What You Change

It might be hard to stay committed when the journey is long. You get stuff done every day and yet change is hardly noticeable. By adding more indicators you'll be able to identify and track how you are spending your time and the results you are getting, which will make it easier to keep on pushing.

Start tracking your time and results at the beginning of each project and do it for each task so you can have a good reference and gather high-quality data. Sometimes, big changes happen at the start, then slow down and then accelerate again.

So when you are at the beginning of what you anticipate will be a long journey, take a second to think about what metrics to track. Start tracking and identify a realistic target.

Record your evolution regularly. The best way is to do it daily. Fill out a classic excel spreadsheet or better, use a notebook.

Just the action of tracking your time and measuring your progress every day should put you on a good path and keep you motivated.

If you're not progressing fast enough or the project isn't going how you expected, change what you're doing. And keep on iterating until you reach your goal.

25

Talk to People

Before writing an email, try to communicate with them directly either in person or by phone.

When communicating by email, it is impossible to convey emotions and to set the proper tone for a conversation. You might sound demanding, or angry where you're not. On the other hand, when you're truly upset, a discussion in person or over the phone might help you to understand what's happening and why and will get you a better result than sending an email that may be interpreted inappropriately or misunderstood.

The more distance and asynchronization you

add to your communications with the people you work with, the greater the risk of lack of understanding and tension.

26

Have Coffee with Colleagues but Not Too Often

Social interactions are very important, specifically at work. Being connected to your ecosystem is the only way to take the pulse of the team and to spot any tiny signals before they become larger issues and/or problems.

The best way to connect is over coffee (one could also say cigarette breaks but I disapprove of smoking).

Every day, take a coffee or a tea mug and spend a couple of minutes with your mates. Share what's on your mind. Listen to what they have to say, be genuinely empathic. You never now, they might help you and you might help them.

But be careful, hanging around the coffee machine can quickly suck up all your time before you realize it. Good ideas might begin there, but they are delivered elsewhere.

27

Have Lunch

The complete rule is: have lunch with other people.

Both parts are important: have lunch, with other people.

Lunch time allows you to take a longer break and get away from work for a while during your workday. It's important you give your brain some downtime to breathe. Eating a salad at your desk while you continue typing on your keyboard doesn't make you someone important. Fun fact, have you noticed that the higher ranked someone is in an organization, the more frequently they get out of the office for lunch?

Lunch is also the time to get some inspiration. Having lunch with your coworkers allows you to deepen the conversation you started at the coffee machine. Having lunch with people outside your organization or with friends will help you get a different perspective on your work.

Lunch time is your opportunity to let off some steam. Let go of the stress from your busy morning. Take the time to recharge your mind. You'll return to your desk refreshed with more energy to tackle your next task.

28

Family and Friendships Have Their Place on Your To-Do List

Personal and professional lives are complementary. There is no hope for long-term self-realization if one side is neglected or undervalued.

Many people are unbalanced. They try to under-invest in one and over-invest in the other. At some point, they realize they are unhappy and they try to reverse their priorities, creating another unbalanced situation. And so on. Whatever your professional ambitions or personal ideals, I strongly advise you to strive for equilibrium as early in your career as possible. That way, you'll continue prioritizing a healthy balance between work and home life and you'll never have to make extreme adjustments that all too commonly end in divorce or mental health issues such as depression or anxiety when one devotes too much energy to their work.

Anyone who is 100% focused on work without any time with their family or friends can not turn well.

Look at your to-do list, the balance between professional and personal items should reflect the way you want to manage your life.

29

Don't Bring Your Work Home

Some people see bringing work home as a sign they are indispensable and they have too many responsibilities. Others see it as a sign of poor organization and time-management. In either case it's not healthy.

It's ok to have some peak activity times during the year and to have to use your computer in the evening on occasion once the kids are in bed. However, this must remain an exception to the rule of leaving your work at work.

During the 24 hours we each have every day, there's time for work, there's time for family, connection and disconnection, and there's time for sleep. When you extend your work hours beyond what's reasonable, you neglect one or two of the other priority areas.

When there's too much on your plate, a good practice is to re-prioritize, with the help of your boss if necessary. If you don't eventually it will lead to burn-out.

30

Take Breaks

After physical exercise, your body needs to rest.

After a sprint, you need to rest for a couple of minutes.
After a 10k run, you need to rest for a couple of days.
After a marathon, you need to rest for a couple of weeks.
And so on.

It's the same for your brain.
After a productive work session, you need a couple of minutes to relax.
After a great day at work, you need to relax

at home or get outside.

After an intense week, you need time to take a break and enjoy your weekend.

Not being able to disconnect and missing out on sufficient time in an ideal decompression chamber is the best way to explode in mid-air.

31

Practice a Sport

Making time to play a sport or get some physical activity is often our last priority. It's there, on the list but everything else comes before.

We often overestimate the time it requires. It's not that hard to plug a 45 minute slot of physical activity into your agenda: 30 minutes of exercise plus 15 minutes to shower. And there are a lot of sports that take only 30 minutes to get an efficient workout: running, swimming, the gym, yoga and so on. Sure, you won't win the Olympics, but you'll get some good natural dopamine.

Do that twice a week: once during the workweek and once during the weekend, and you're good.

Each session will help you free your mind and make space for new ideas, new inspirations for home and for work.
Being fit will obviously help you live a longer, better quality life and help you better cope with stressful situations.

32

Sleep

Most of us need six to eight hours of sleep every night. There are exceptions. There are people who sleep just four or five hours per night and they are perfectly fine.

Parents of young children are the best example of how lack of sleep impacts your day-to-day life. You are less focused, less patient and less productive. There's no happy ending when you continue cutting off minutes of sleep that your mind and body desperately need.

When we don't get enough sleep, we are Zombies. Zombies are easy to spot: they walk around with a coffee mug in their hand and their face is blank when they look at you or stare at their computer screen.

It's not hard to guess that Zombies are not productive.

Find your sweet spot, don't force yourself to wake-up every morning at 5am unless you develop a routine to go to sleep at 9pm. If you don't get enough sleep, eventually you'll become a Zombie who is eventually unable to focus for more than ten seconds.

33

Take Vacations

Vacations are not just a long break from work. Vacations are a total disconnection from your daily habits and routines. It's not only about work having time away from work. It's a global reboot of your system.

Up to three times a year, at least once a year, you must take real vacations. Pack your bags, take your car, a train or a plane and go live somewhere else for at least a week. Discover new places, new products, new leisure activities.

If you're still at home, it's not a vacation, it's just a long break from the office.

The act of disconnection from work and from the stress and projects to do at home allows you to reconnect with yourself, your family and your life. It's the only way to reframe your purpose and update your priorities.

34

Celebrate

There's no such thing as a small victory.

Every achievement, no matter how big or how small, deserves a true celebration. We tend to celebrate only big victories. These might only happen once or twice a year. And we tend to want to make it such a big deal that it's a burden to organize.
On the other hand, we're quickly bothered by small issues, worries and roadblocks.

We're not used to celebrating weekly successes. Take a moment to think about your last ten days, I am sure there was a small achievement, or good news to celebrate. It's highly likely that someone from your family or your team did something great in the past week. Take a moment to recognize it. Don't just offer the team kudos at the coffee machine. Go out for a drink after work or organize a celebration lunch outside the office.

35

Don't Read Too Many Books

Now close this book, take the knowledge and skills you've gained along the way by absorbing the wisdom behind the rules and go do amazing things in the world. It needs you.

The more time you spend reading, the less time you are spending creating, building and delivering. Sure, books have things to teach, messages to pass on. But you also have your own story to write.

There is a time to read books, and there's a

time to write them.

36

There is No Big Decision, Only Small Ones

Many people believe that their live will be marked by a few big decisions that will determine their future. That's not true.

Some of these decisive moments do exist. But our fate is deeply shaped by the myriad of small choices we make every day, every hour, indeed every minute.

"Do I take a break, or do I work on that analysis that's been sitting in my to-do list for weeks?"

"Do I open a new file, or do I go to pick up my kids from school?"

"Do I indulge in dessert, or do I stick to my diet?"

There is often no good or bad answer to that kind of question. Even if you're an athlete, you can take a cheat meal sometimes and go for the donut. But if you make that decision every other meal, there's few chances you'll reach the top league.

You must be aware that almost all day long you face minor decision that, compounded, could have significant consequences in the future. Don't wait for a big decision to prove your commitment to a cause or to your priorities. Every minute is an occasion to do it.

37

Be Curious

Curiosity is a powerful force that constantly drives us to discover new ideas, concepts, and practices.
It enriches us and allows us to develop our impact.

Children, with their innate curiosity, aspire daily to acquire new skills that are essential for their growth and development. I am convinced that maintaining our curiosity keeps us young, acting like the much-sought-after fountain of youth.

It is vital to remain in awe of the world, always listening and seeking what can stimulate our development and progress.

So, dare to step off the beaten path, leave your comfort zone, and try new experiences. This is how we learn and continue to grow and evolve.

38

Be Inspired by People

Every interaction with someone is an opportunity to learn something.

Some people are very charismatic and naturally inspiring. Beyond these extraordinary individuals that we come across only a few times in a lifetime, every day we meet people who possess strengths and can be a great source of development.

When you interact with someone, take a genuine interest in their personality. Try to identify what he or she does differently from you, both in the way of working and in the way of being. Understand the type of impact that this person has on the world and identify where they do better than you, in their work, with their team, or with their family.

Once you have found what makes the persons in front of you extraordinary, from the doorman of your building to the executives in your company, let yourself be taught by them. Turn each of your encounters into a private lesson, even if you never tell them.

39

Seek feedback

It is challenging to have a relevant and insightful understanding of one's impact.

The only way to gauge your performance and identify your development areas is to seek feedback from the people you interact with.

The end of each cycle (project, quarter, year, job change) is a good opportunity to invite your interlocutors to share their thoughts on your work and to suggest areas for improvement. The approach can be more or less formal and extensive. At the very least, take the time to discuss with your hierarchical or functional manager as well as with some of your closest collaborators.

Most of the time, there are formal annual evaluations in companies with your boss, but I suggest doing this exercise more regularly throughout the year and in a more friendly manner.

Personally, what I also appreciate and find very beneficial is to ask for small feedbacks almost every day. For example, after a meeting in which I have presented something, I immediately ask my boss or someone from my team how the intervention was perceived and how it could have had a greater impact.

Then, it's up to you to note these areas for improvement and identify the best way to progress.

Special Bonus Rule

Be Ambitious but Pragmatic

In this book, I've focused on the how, not on the what and the why. Those are up to you. Your purpose, your goals are your own.

The only trap I would like to warn you about is the one of vain wish. You can be anything you want in this world. Really. There are plenty of stories of people born in the street becoming movie stars, super athletes, or CEOs of big companies.

Go after the stars. Set your goals as high possible. But then you must commit to them. Think logically, imagine the steps you'll have to take.

Want to be a rockstar? Fine, buy a guitar at a pawnshop for $20, then begin to learn how to play it and sing. Don't spend your time on the PlayStation.

Want to reach C-level of your company? Fine, talk to your boss, get some training, volunteer for new projects. Don't stay at your desk waiting for someone to come and invite you. If you want it, get started today and do the work.

There's no favorable winds for the ship without a destination.

Have an ambition, have at least a vague idea of how you could get there and start today.

Printed in Great Britain
by Amazon

40909909R00059